Six Steps to Quality

How to Plan and Implement A
Continuous Quality Improvement
Program for
Colleges and Universities.

by

Robert A. Cornesky, Sc.D.

CORNESKY & ASSOCIATES, INC.
489 Oakland Park Blvd.
Port Orange, Florida 32127
Phone: (800) 388-8682 or (904) 760-5866
Fax: (904) 756-6755

E-Mail: TQM1BOB@AOL.COM

First Printing August 1996

ISBN 1-881087-13-4

TABLE OF CONTENTS

INTRODUCTION

s a college or university administrator, you are always looking for ways to improve your services, cut costs and yet maintain your institution's high standards. As consultants, we have devoted more than a decade to helping administrators like you achieve those goals by understanding and applying Continuous Quality Improvement (CQI) ideas. While CQI was born in industry, it is not restricted to behind factory walls. We bring to your attention those steps that you might want to consider to help you apply basic CQI principles to most campuses.

The process borrows extensively from recognized leaders in the quality field and encourages you to develop your own quality improvement model based on your institution's particular mission.

Using CQI procedures, you and your colleagues will constantly examine how things are being done and look for ways to improve the processes and systems. That effort will evolve into better service that leads to increased customer satisfaction and reduced costs.

Cornesky & Associates, Inc. • (800) 388-8682

Purpose of this booklet

This booklet explains CQI and recommends that six steps be considered before implementing CQI at any college or university.

What is CQI?

CQI is a philosophy that encourages everyone in your institution to know its mission and to adopt quality-driven procedures that continuously improve on how the work is done in order to increase customer satisfaction. The general principles of CQI encourages all employees—from the President to clerks—to point out processes and systems that are not working properly and to recommend improvements. CQI encourages teamwork and shuns inflexible rules and regulations.

**Good is not good
where better
is expected.
Thomas Fuller**

How is higher education different?

The CQI that has found a home in business cannot be transferred directly into academe. As famed educator John D. Millett (1962) noted:

> *The internal organization of a college or university does not resemble that of the Army and Navy, or the Department of Agriculture, or of the Atomic Energy Commission, or of the Federal Trade Commission, or of the Department of Sanitation in a large municipality. The internal organization of a college or university does not resemble that of a steel mill company, a department store, a bank, or a hotel. Colleges and universities are different. They are different in institutional setting, in purpose, in operation, and hence in internal organization.*

Honest differences are often a healthy sign of progress. Mahatma Gandhi

Higher education traditionally has been guided by three primary purposes:

1) teaching,
2) research, and
3) service.

Colleges and universities gather, transmit, and store knowledge. That's not a formula for financial success. Academe spends money; it almost never earns much. However, our children need to be educated to further advance themselves, society and our economic base. Part of the function of education, therefore, is to expand the ability of people to produce goods and services. It follows that education is an investment in human beings just as tools are an investment for a plant producing a product.

**Great minds have purposes, others have wishes.
Washington Irving**

What do faculty think about applying the principles of CQI?

None of that usually means anything to many faculty members who are convinced that the goal of the academic community is to provide the environment for learning, not a product of learning. As a result, instructors may be teaching, but students may not be learning.

Understandable, faculty argue that knowledge is not like an automobile, a piece of furniture, a house, or any product that is manufactured. However, such an argument turns the faculty member into the final customer, not the student. Under that approach, your instructors may be satisfied while your students are not. CQI shifts the perspective: students, as the final customer, must demonstrate they have learned. Only then can faculty members prove they have taught.

To shift perspectives, faculty must realize their classrooms contain four different systems:

1) facilitating or teaching;
2) learning;
3) CQI; and
4) reward.

When they make that switch, they become thought-leaders; their students learn more; classroom procedures are constantly assessed and improved; and teaching and learning become fun .

Why must we improve our system of higher education?

You are probably wondering why colleges and universities should consider CQI at all. Doesn't the United States enjoy the best higher education system in the world? It certainly has enabled our country to become the world leader and to maintain that position. Americans have won the majority of Nobel Prizes; we have educated a greater proportion of our young people than any other nation; and we attract students from around the world to our colleges and universities. Still, our productivity is not increasing at the same rate as in Japan and Germany. Our high school students do not do as well in science, math, and reading comprehension than their international counterparts. What's wrong? Why do we have the best scientists and so many students that do poorly in science, the best business schools and yet a lagging economy with a declining competitive edge? Why do we have such a high attrition rate in our institutions of higher education? Can we say we are really educating if so many students are not learning?

We certainly can't let education continue to slide, not as demand for educated employees increases. Top educators know that. William B. Johnson (1987) pointed out that education is increasingly important since all new jobs developed by the year 2000 will require at least some postsecondary education. Education is also playing a primary role in economic transitions. Colin Norman (1988) stated ... *the changes underway in the economy are placing an unprecedented demand on the intellectual skills and knowledge of American workers.*

Derek Bok (1990) added ... *all advanced nations depend increasingly on three critical elements: new discoveries, highly trained personnel, and expert knowledge. In America, universities are primarily responsible for supplying two of these ingredients and are a major source for the third.* (p. 3)

CQI remains the best method for boosting educational results and helping this country remain the world's economic leader.

**I place economy among the first and most important virtues, and public debt as the greatest of dangers...
Thomas Jefferson**

CORNESKY & ASSOCIATES, INC. • (800) 388-8682

THE SIX STEPS FOR IMPLEMENTING CQI

We suggest that you consider six steps before implementing CQI in your institution. These are listed below with a brief summary. This booklet will devote a chapter to each step.

1) Educate the administration

Senior management must acquire a shared appreciation and understanding of Continuous Quality Improvement (CQI) concepts. This can be done in the course of a three-day retreat. At the retreat, the President must show how proposed plans and implementation actions will result in desired quality improvements.

2) Establish the commitment of the administration

Senior management must develop a plan to introduce CQI concepts to the campus community, including an implementation schedule and identification of target audiences.

3) Establish quality awareness

Senior management must develop a comprehensive, progressive training program aimed at educating employees at all levels to support the program.

4) Establish baseline data

One of the main functions of CQI is to show constant improvement in the quality of service and product delivered. Therefore, measurements must be done in all departments to gather baseline data and then repeated at a later time to see if your processes and systems are improving.

5) Set goals

Once the data is gathered, the institution can set improvement goals.

6) Establish a recognition program

The process is enhanced by recognizing employees who develop quality ideas and boost productivity and customer satisfaction. Any recognition ceremony, which probably shouldn't be initiated for two or more years after starting the CQI effort, should include representatives from both inside your institution and from major suppliers (high schools and community colleges) and customers (employers). In addition to the faculty, staff, and administration, the President should include students from major student-based organizations, as well as their parents and political representatives from the city or region.

A leader has to be a reflection of the soul of the organization.
Philip B. Crosby

CHAPTER ONE

Educate
The
Administration

Y our President and top managers must undertake a training program on the principles of CQI before making a concerted effort to apply them throughout the institution. You'll be making major changes; you can't convince your fellow managers to alter their traditional management style if they don't completely understand the process.

Everyone needs to learn the same information—President, managers from all academic and non-academic units including the Deans, Directors and Department Chairs. Your governing board and CQI advisory councils should attend a similar workshop.

At minimum, we recommend that the following five topics be included during the three-day retreat. Each topic should include case studies from other institutions that attempted to implement CQI. In the back of this booklet, you'll find sources listed. In each chapter we'll list the numbers of the sources you can check for additional guidance.

TOPIC 1:
Approaches to
Continuous Quality Improvement

The purpose of this topic is to introduce the administration to the approaches of CQI by reviewing the ideas of quality leaders and discussing how their ideas might apply to your institution and its mission. We suggest that you discuss philosophies developed by Crosby, Deming, Juran, and Imai. See readings 7, 8, 10, 11, 15, 19, 24, 27, 35, and 42.

TOPIC 2:
Principles of
Continuous Quality Improvement

The purpose of this topic is to examine the common elements introduced by the various quality experts and discuss how they might be applied to your institution and its mission. The common elements that should be discussed are:

1) processes and systems,
2) teaming,
3) customers and suppliers,
4) quality by fact, of process, and by perception,
5) management by fact,
6) complexity, and
7) variation.

See readings 4, 5, 8, 10, 11, 14, and 39.

TOPIC 3:
Applying the
Malcolm Baldrige Criteria
to Measure Quality

The purpose of this topic is to discuss the nationally recognized procedure encapsulated in the Malcolm Baldrige National Quality Award (MBNQA) Education Pilot Criteria to measure the quality of your institution and its mission. The MBNQA Education Pilot Criteria creates quality standards that provide a target for any educational institution. It includes the following categories:

1) leadership,
2) information and analysis,
3) strategic and operational planning,
4) human resource development and management,
5) education and business process management,
6) school performance results, and
7) student focus and student and stakeholder satisfaction.

See readings 8, 11, 13, 40, and 41.

TOPIC 4:
The Plan-Do-Check-Act Cycle

The purpose of this topic is to introduce the Plan-Do-Check-Act (PDCA) cycle, a fundamental CQI process. Training and discussions should be conducted on:

1) how to identify problems contributing to non value-added work,
2) how to construct effective teams,
3) how to pinpoint the root causes of problems rather than symptoms, and
4) procedures for implementing suggested improvements generated by your teams (12).

Action to be effective must be directed to clearly conceived needs. Jawaharial Nehry

CORNESKY & ASSOCIATES, INC. • (800) 388-8682

TOPIC 5:
Continuous Quality Improvement
Tools and Techniques

The purpose of this topic is to explain the CQI tools and techniques commonly used to assess the quality of your processes and systems. Eventually, these tools will be used by the quality improvement teams to identify root causes of problems and to make recommendations for improvements. In time, administrators should be able to use and/or understand the following tools:

1)   affinity diagram,
2)   cause-and-effect diagram,
3)   control charts,
4)   flow charts,
5)   histograms,
6)   nominal group process,
7)   operational definition,
8)   Pareto Diagram,
9)   relations diagram,
10) run chart,
11) scatter diagram,
12) scenario builder, and the
13) systematic diagram.

See readings 9, 10, 11, 12, 33, 37, and 38.

At the end of this first step toward implementing quality improvement, you should have an administration educated in the philosophy of CQI.

Quality is never an accident; it is always the result of high intention, sincere effort, intelligent direction and skillful execution; it represents the wise choice of many alternatives. Willa A. Foster

If it is going to be practical and achievable, quality management must start at the top.

Philip B. Crosby

Establish The Commitment of The Administration

CHAPTER TWO

ow it's time for the President and top administrators to introduce CQI concepts—including an implementation schedule and identification of target audiences—to the campus community. Managers must do much more than make an announcement that the institution will be converting to a quality philosophy. Your President must work with the senior managers to accomplish the following understandings. See readings 15, 35, and 36.

Make it apparent that CQI is not being tested as a concept

Employees must know that CQI is being implemented throughout the entire institution. As pointed out by Peters and Austin in *A Passion for Excellence* (1985), *[a]ttention to quality can become the organization's mind-set only if **all** of its managers—indeed, all of its people—live it.* They stress that to "live it" means paying attention to quality 100 percent of the time and not allowing occasional lapses.

Appoint a Vice President for
Continuous Quality Improvement

You probably think the first step your institution should take is to hire a CQI Coordinator. You may want to rethink that. Why? Because the CQI Coordinator post has become isolated, often filled with individuals with the wrong kind of background who are receiving minimal salaries and even less administrative support. That's definitely a recipe for anything but quality.

After all, at this stage, your institution probably does not have an institutional policy on quality. Without the active support of campus leaders, the CQI Coordinator can do little to influence the cultural change that is necessary to undertake the transformation to a better quality institution. The end result is that neither quality nor the CQI Coordinator is perceived as really being important.

Many CQI Coordinators quickly become irrelevant for another reason: they have been trained in an industrial setting and know next to nothing about the operation of an academic institution. They do know how to facilitate functional and cross-functional teams and how to use a variety of CQI tools and techniques, but understand little about the processes and systems in the classrooms and still less about curriculum development and teaching/learning strategies. That often creates a chasm between the CQI Coordinator and the school that no quality plan can bridge.

In addition, the CQI Coordinator position itself may even have a detrimental affect on work morale. Faculty and staff, who should have the responsibility of evaluating quality, may start seeing the person who holds the CQI

Coordinator title not as a partner or facilitator, but rather as a judge. As a result, the CQI Coordinator often ends up not only managing by fact, but also becoming a behaviorist who must overcome fears, appease egos and continually recognize the accomplishments of people, especially faculty.

How many coordinators have sufficient training for that complex role?

Low salaries are adding to the burden. The CQI Coordinator is rarely considered an important or influential person on most campuses, especially since most CQI Coordinators are near the bottom in prestige and income.

Still, you will need someone to head your school's quality effort, especially with the ever increasing societal demand that educational institutions improve their quality standards. Instead, the position is being twisted into a different shape under intense pressure from faculty and staff. The new role will allow CQI Coordinators to continue to have an important place in colleges but with a different function.

The person responsible for quality processes and systems will not watch from outside. Rather, as colleges flatten their internal organizational structures, the assignment of quality professionals to a specific department will be replaced by project teams capable of handling most process problems.

The function of a CQI Coordinator will then evolve from training and data collecting to a very important one of data interpretation and application. And, most importantly, these leaders will enjoy a greater latitude of action while helping maintain the quality movement in higher education.

We recommend, therefore, that the President appoint a **Vice President for Continuous Quality Improvement**, rather than a Coordinator, no later than within six months after initiating the CQI effort.

The Vice President for CQI should have extensive experience as both a **faculty** member and an **administrator** in an institution of higher education. We recommend that this executive be totally familiar with the principles and procedures of CQI, and that the job description include the following duties (modified from Boedecker, 1989):

- Develop and teach quality-awareness programs for all personnel.

- Constantly survey the employees to pinpoint task, process, and system problems requiring improvement.

- Educate the CQI quality advisory councils (see below) appointed by the President as well as the community advisory council, and members of the governing board.

- Promote the customer/supplier concept throughout the institution.

- Meet with external "customers" to understand their perceptions of the institution.

- Encourage the integration of process and system designs with emphasis on error-free processes.

- Recommend the allocation of resources to properly meet process and system requirements.

- Establish detection methods that isolate process and system errors.

- Establish benchmarking and statistical techniques for the various divisions/units.

- Coordinate the development of the institution's long-term strategy towards CQI.

- Publish a newsletter that communicates CQI successes (and failures).

- Post graphs and charts showing CQI trends for various departments/units.

- Manage the CQI center/institute as described below.

Appoint a CQI community advisory council

Your President will need the assistance of a CQI advisory council, comprised of **suppliers** (such as high school educators) and **customers** (such as employers of the graduates, parents of students or even the students themselves). We recommend that the CQI advisory council receive the same training as described in Chapter One, either at the same time the upper administration does, or with the training sessions for mid-level managers.

The training is important because it reduces barriers and provides the necessary background in CQI ideas. By bringing the external groups with their varying perspectives together, the council not only acts as a barometer of public opinion about your institution, but also provides valuable information as how better to guide your institution's CQI efforts.

He that won't be counselled can't be helped Benjamin Franklin

CORNESKY & ASSOCIATES, INC. • (800) 388-8682

Appoint a CQI advisory council
for each unit/department

We recommend creating a separate CQI advisory council for each academic area. It should consist of professionals from the community, the department chairpersons and the Dean. Councils should be expected to hold regular meetings that are devoted entirely to CQI and should be required to report monthly on their achievements to the Vice President for CQI. Quality meetings should be as important as any other departmental gathering.

These CQI councils should be expected to:

1) Focus the unit's quality processes towards desired objectives that are consistent with the institution's mission and long-range goals.

2) Ensure that the CQI education is adequate and ongoing.

3) Do continual reviews and benchmarking and display quality-improvement trends in forms of graphs and charts.

4) Use CQI procedures to constantly prioritize and update those tasks, processes, and systems that appear to be adding to the cost of nonquality.

5) Encourage participation of all employees in quality-improvement teams.

6) Recognize quality improvements internally and externally.

7) Identify and correct tasks, processes, and systems that detract from a quality education and/or experience.

It takes nearly as much ability to know how to profit by good advice as to know how to act for one's self.
Francois de La Rochefoucauld

Encourage members of the governing board
to undergo CQI training

You can't overlook your governing board. Members will need to attend an in-depth training session at least once a year as most members come from the traditional business and educational settings which do not really practice CQI. They need to understand and appreciate CQI reports and terminology.

Once your board members become convinced of the value of CQI, they will serve as ardent supporters of your efforts and as advocates with the community and the legislature. This support could lead to increased funding.

Finally, after CQI is implemented, board members will very likely insist that future presidents and senior managers completely understand CQI and are committed to it. Since members of the governing board usually serve as a link between the institution and the employers, they could be instrumental in getting everyone involved in the transformation to quality.

Education is a
progressive discovery
of our ignorance.
Will Durant

Have a management team write a
quality philosophy guide book

After the President and the governing board have established a vision statement of what they would like their institution to be within the next decade, the President should instruct a top management team to write a quality philosophy handbook. This project should be coordinated by the Vice President for CQI as a continuous "work-in-progress." It gives employees a text which they can refer to and revise, and provides an important sense of participation rather than being subject to a process.

The importance of this guidebook should not be underestimated. It should clearly and succinctly state the institutional mission and the importance of quality in delivering the educational experience.

Quality improvement has no chance unless the individuals are ready to recognize that improvement is necessary.
Philip B. Crosby

Establish a CQI Center/Institute

The next step is to set up a CQI Center. The Center creates a physical setting for what is essentially a series of philosophical ideas, and it advertises that quality is important. The Center can fulfill a variety of key functions, including:

1) act as the educational arm for the administration and for the faculty, and staff;

2) coordinate continuing education activities for the external agencies that request CQI training;

3) act as a broker between the institution and the community it serves;

4) act as a conduit for quality research activities for not only the institution (faculty, administrators, staff), but also for the outside community;

5) help faculty develop quality teaching strategies for the classroom; and,

6) be the source for educating the institution's suppliers and independent contractors.

Make quality improvement an agenda item at performance evaluations

Crosby (1984) states that after the CQI policy has been instituted, usable status reports have to be part of important meetings. To fulfill that guideline, you will need to maintain constant performance evaluations based on quality concepts and make quality a regular part of meetings between the President and the senior administrators. They should maintain a close watch on the following:

1)   *The quality improvement process*
   - *How many employees have been educated?*
   - *Are the teams functioning properly?*
   - *What success stories do we have to share?*
   - *What problems need action?*

2)   *The cost of quality*
   - *Do we have the format in all operations?*
   - *What are the trends?*
   - *Where do the biggest improvement opportunities lie?*
   - *What problems need action?*

3)   *Conformance*
   - *Are we meeting our requirements?*
   - *What actions do we have to take to emphasize the need to meet them?*

Establish and measure quality goals

Your institution will have to review constantly its progress regarding *the quality improvement process, the cost of quality, and its conformance toward meeting goals.* To achieve this end, we suggest that the management be trained in Hoshin Planning (37).

It is obvious that progress towards CQI must begin with the support of the President and the top management since they control the allocation of resources. If they set an example for the rest of the institution, Deans, Chairs, and Directors will quickly recognize that the movement is authentic and not just the latest fad. The faculty and staff will eventually accept the fact that the CQI movements are not just another method to increase productivity but a very real commitment towards **quality**.

That doesn't mean faculty and staff may not feel threatened by the CQI effort. That can be overcome by establishing trust outside some artificial time commitment. It will take time to create that trust and to develop pride-in-workmanship and an increase in quality. Eventually, though, a new institutional culture will be established. See readings 20, 30, and 43.

In summary, the first step to implementing CQI in an institution of higher education is to educate the management. The second step is to have management take a leadership role by making a firm commitment towards CQI.

When it's a pleasure to come to work because the requirements for quality are taken seriously and management is helpful, then attitudes change permanently.
Philip B. Crosby

Great minds must be ready not only to take opportunities, but to make them.

Colton

*Establish
Quality
Awareness*

e believe that quality awareness is best approached by first educating the employees about the principles of CQI techniques and then have them use their training to take corrective action, remove causes of errors in processes and systems, and participate in quality councils and teams.

Educate the employees

Critical to the success of CQI is the education of managers along with faculty and staff. Once the faculty and staff understand the principles of CQI, they will commit to the movement even if only in incremental amounts. The education of faculty and staff should include an understanding of 1) teaming, 2) quality philosophies and processes, as well as training in the 3) Plan-Do-Check-Act or PDCA cycle and on the 4) tools and techniques that they will need in order to implement CQI. It will be necessary to separate the various departments and to tailor the programs for each unit, such as the academic departments, the accounting department, continuing education, the police department, building and grounds, etc.

The obvious reason for educating the employees on CQI is to inform them that their participation is essential for the processes to work. After they realize that their contributions are respected and their responsibilities for improving the quality are essential, most employees will make a commitment. If, after they receive training, employees return to the office and discover that they cannot change systems and processes because they do not have the necessary resources or support to implement what they have learned, the CQI movement will fail as the frustration level increases.

Crosby states (1984, p. 111) that quality has to become part of the corporate culture. Everyone should understand that management is committed to quality, and, therefore, quality is the policy. He emphasizes that the employees must be informed on the cost of not doing a task correctly the first time. (What are the real costs to society when a university fails to graduate a competent student?)

You cannot expect anyone to do anything for which they have not been educated or trained to do.
Robert A. Cornesky

Establish quality councils

Crosby (1984) points out that *[t]he idea of quality councils is to bring the quality professionals together and let them learn from each other* (p. 119). This is an excellent way in which to keep the organization focused on "quality" issues and to prevent slippage back to the traditional manner of operation. "Quality councils" are truly a necessity to ensure that the institution's subcultures are pointed in the same direction since many managers and faculty often believe that CQI programs are not really applicable to their units.

The only thing to do with good advice is to pass it on.
Oscar Wilde

Establish quality improvement teams

Forming effective improvement teams is central to CQI. A main purpose of improvement teams is to identify problems and then to take the corrective actions necessary to eliminate their reoccurrence. Corrective action does not consist of redoing someone else's mistakes but may involve identifying suppliers who are not meeting conformance standards and then communicating precisely what you expect from their product or service. The supplier might be external such as the local high school, or internal such as the English Department that passes a student who does not have the terminal competencies required to write a clear composition.

In order to get everyone involved in adopting the new quality philosophy Crosby (1984, p. 106) clearly states that the organization must form quality improvement teams (QIT), consisting of individuals who represent all functions of the organization. The QIT's are more than inter-disciplinary committees. In higher education, **cross-functional teams** are rare: secretaries, custodial personnel, human relations personnel, building and grounds personnel, police, faculty, management, union officers, alumni, board members, employers of the graduates, and students are rarely placed on a team to do anything. One can only speculate what would happen on most campuses if such teams were established routinely in order to implement a CQI culture on campus.

Crosby says the CQI team should:

1) have clear directions for its purpose to guide, coordinate, and support the entire quality implementation process;

2) have power to clear obstacles and to commit resources;

3) primarily be concerned with setting up of educational activities; and that

4) the chairperson of the team should have direct and easy access to the President.

We recommend that all administrators be a part of quality improvement teams if for no other reason than the activity will constantly remind them of the importance of the quality effort to identify poor systems and to take corrective action steps. This should result in people concentrating on improving poor tasks, processes, and systems and less on blaming and finger pointing.

The second step in the quality improvement effort combines the interrelationship between using the education acquired in the first two steps with **teaming** in order to identify poor **processes and systems** prior to taking corrective action. Let's examine the principles of teaming and processes and systems.

Teaming

Teams and teamwork are extremely important in the process of producing a quality service or product. Although hierarchy is needed within all organizations to avoid chaos, most work in universities is accomplished across, not within, organizational boundaries. This cross-functional process model is shown in the figure below.

Cross-functional model for processing work.

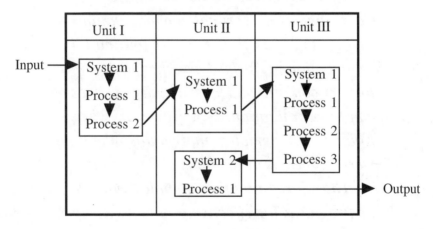

According to Hrebiniak (1978, p. 137):

> . . . *in organizations with strong hierarchical and status differences, communications will be vertical in nature, and often biased. Top-level personnel make important decisions and lower-level personnel implement them. This results in a predominantly up-down flow of task-related information. The respect for people of higher status may result in a reluctance to criticize their ideas, and cause the transmission of information that subordinates feel superiors would like to hear.*
>
> *The emphasis on vertical communications further suggests that the tall pyramidal organization performs best when tasks are not very complex and most activity involves simple coordination. . . . However, when problems are complex, individuals may be overwhelmed by the quantity of information. . . . Thus, for nonroutine, complex matters, the prognosis for effective problem solving in the hierarchical system does not appear to be a good one.*

The informal power structure and the resulting culture in colleges and universities do not readily permit collegiality in a management system based upon hierarchy; however, teaming, when done properly, is invariably found in colleges and universities having high morale.

In their recent books, Waterman (1990) and Levering (1988) stress the importance of teamwork in effecting change and in keeping morale high.

Waterman says that a well-run project team can . . . *cut across conventional lines and boundaries* [and is] *designed to effect change* (p. 6). He states that a well-run project team solves the problem of lousy implementation, one of management's most common problems. However, he does not believe that bureaucracy should be destroyed, but that it must coexist with adhocracy (any organizational form that promotes collegial rather than bureaucratic behavior).

Levering says that being part of a team represents a risk, but that *people cannot thrive unless they have some say in how much they wish to contribute* (p. 217). He also stresses that all employees should have the right to full and accurate data, the right to free and open speech without the fear of reprisal, and a stake in the results.

Selecting processes that if improved will greatly advance the quality of service provided is one of the best and most highly recommended ways in which to approach changes towards an organizational culture of CQI. Waterman (1990), in his powerful book *Adhocracy: The Power to Change*, refers to means for getting people actively involved in embracing and effecting change. He suggests that people, under the proper leadership, will participate in meaningful task forces with the intention of changing their organization from one of non-quality to one of high quality.

An excellent way of helping people to embrace change is to identify the causes that detract from doing quality work. This may be done by using one or more of the tools listed in the following table (see readings 9, 10, 11, 12, and 33).

The world hates change, yet it is the only thing that has brought progress. Charles F. Kettering

SEVERAL EXTREMELY USEFUL
CONTINUOUS QUALITY IMPROVEMENT TOOLS THAT CAN BE USED
TO IDENTIFY AND RANK
"PROCESSES" AND/OR "SYSTEMS" PROBLEMS.

Affinity Diagram
- Used to examine complex and/or hard to understand problems
- Used to build team consensus
- Results can be further analyzed by a **Relations Diagram**

Cause and Effect Diagram (Fishbones)
- Used to identify **root causes** of a problem
- Used to draw out many ideas and/or opinions about the causes

Flow Charts
- Gives a picture of the process and the system

Force Field Analysis
- Used when changing the system might be difficult and/or complex

Histogram
- A bar graph of data which displays information about the data set and shape
- Can be used to predict the stability in the system

Nominal Group Process
- A structured process to help groups make decisions
- Useful in choosing a problem to work on
- Used to build team consensus
- Used to draw out many ideas and/or opinions about the causes

Pareto Diagram
- Bar chart that ranks data by categories
- Used to show that a few items contribute greatly to the overall problem
- Helps the team identify which processes/systems to direct their efforts

Relations Diagram
- Helps the team to analyze the cause and effect relationships between factors
- Directs the team to the **root** causes of a problem

Systematic Diagram
- Used when a broad task or goal becomes the focus of the team's work
- Often used after an **Affinity Diagram** and/or **Relations Diagram**
- Used when the action plan is needed to accomplish the goal

Once a problem has been identified and a quality improvement team established, the team must gather and analyze data from the processes and systems contributing to the perceived problem. After suggestions are recommended and implemented to rectify the problem, the processes and systems are standardized, evaluated, and plans for continuous improvement are implemented. This is graphically illustrated in the following figure that shows a flow chart of a PDCA cycle.

Never, Never, Never Quit!
Winston Churchill

A Flow Chart of a Plan-Do-Check-Act Cycle

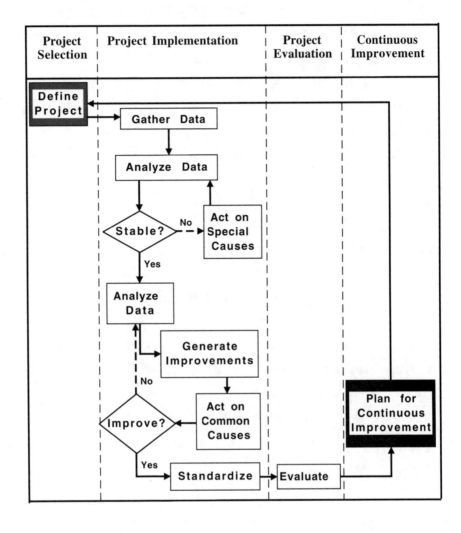

Cornesky & Associates, Inc. • (800) 388-8682

One effective way of getting input about the causes of the identified problems in the processes and systems is to post **cause-and-effect** diagrams, known also as fishbone charts and Ishikawa Diagrams. Since most problems have more than one cause, the cause-and-effect diagram is useful in showing the relationships between a problem and multiple causes. They are most effective if the employees who contributed to the initial identification of a problem are asked for their opinion of the causes. The four common main causes of a problem are equipment, procedures, materials, and personnel; however, don't limit the main categories to only these four.

The following figure shows a cause-and-effect diagram with an undesirable, identified problem needing to be resolved. Called an "effect," it could have been identified by one or more of the tools listed above such as the affinity diagram, relations diagram, and/or the nominal group process. As can be seen, the effect can have not only one or more main causes, but also be the result of causes at several levels.

A cause-and-effect diagram showing the
various causes of a problem.

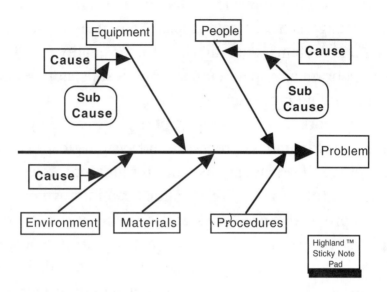

It's a good idea to have a 3 x 4 foot diagram in each administrative office area when trying to clarify the perceptions about various problems. The sign should have **Highland**™ note pads attached so that the written remarks could be added by the associates, secretaries, faculty, students, and anyone else who enters the office. At the end of several weeks, the manager should gather the information and share it, possibly via a newsletter.

Processes and Systems

Many quality leaders stress improving the processes and systems in which employees work in order to improve the quality of goods and services. Deming and Juran stress that since management controls at least 85 percent of the processes and systems, the majority of poor quality results is due to poor management emphasizing results alone rather than improving processes.

Every work activity is a part of a process and system, and there are countless processes and systems that exist in every office. If organizations work through processes and systems, it follows that organizations can improve only if they improve the processes and systems in which the employees work. It also follows that if managers at our universities improve the processes and systems, they will not only get better quality results but they will increase productivity as well.

A "system" as used in this text is an arrangement of persons, places, things, and/or circumstances that either makes, facilitates, or permits things to happen. The very nature of a system will determine what will happen and how it will happen.

Here are several reasons to explain the importance of understanding systems:

1) By knowing a system, it is possible to avoid errors by not permitting the system to try to handle something that it was not designed to handle.

2) By knowing the end product or service function that you are trying to produce or accomplish, you should be able to design and choose a system to produce the product or perform the function. However, although you should be able to predict the outcomes and behavior within a system and thus alter either the outcomes or behavior, you should understand

3) it is not always possible to infer the over-all performance of a system by examining its individual parts. Finally,

4) it is very possible that each of the different units within a complex institution might very well have an efficient system, but the systems between the units may be incompatible.

Since most administrators inherit organizations established by previous managers, they face the challenge of maintaining the strengths and eliminating the weaknesses of existing systems. Commonly, they have entered situations governed by closed systems where anticipated results yield predictable attitudes and behaviors. This cycle of predictability is not only difficult to alter but also inhibits the changing of processes that can lead to better quality.

Since administrators control 85-90 percent of the processes and systems, we are convinced that if they seriously commit to quality, they can influence faculty, staff, and students to do likewise. Faculty and staff will most likely work hard if they are convinced that quality will be the end result. If management directs all of its energies towards improving the processes and systems for quality results with those faculty and staff responsible for providing and receiving the service, we are confident that quality results will end in a modified behavior, a better attitude and eventually an organizational culture directed towards achieving quality.

In summary, the first step to implementing CQI in an institution of higher education is to educate the management. The second step is to have management take a leadership role by making a firm commitment towards CQI. The third step is to establish quality awareness throughout the institution by having the employees educated in CQI, establishing quality advisory councils and quality improvement teams.

We cannot direct the wind... but
we can adjust the sails.
Anonymous

The measurement of quality
is the
price of nonconformance.
                    Philip B. Crosby

*Establish
Baseline
Data*

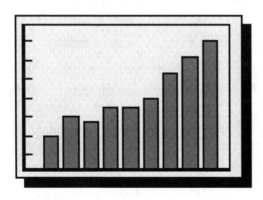

rosby makes the point that gathering baseline data is necessary for evaluating the improvement process. He states that people become frustrated when such data are not available and, as a result, they don't know how they are doing. In fact, he implies that people and organizations become frustrated when they do not have clear performance measurements.

Since one of the main functions of CQI is to show constant improvement in the quality of service and product delivered, measurements must be done in all departments in order to gather baseline data and to assess various operations over time to show that the processes and systems are improving.

Gathering data and pointing out defects initially will be considered a threat by employees—but this is a natural response. The only way to overcome that is to establish trust. In institutions having poor records of collegiality, this may take time. Don't set an artificial deadline; trust requires a long-term relationship (14, 30). When trust exists, the faculty and staff will feel empowered—they have greater control of not only the functions of their job but also can make their jobs more efficient.

The first way to establish trust is to explain in detail why comprehensive measurements have to be taken. Explanations should show how data can:

1) demonstrate trends in customer satisfaction levels, including their satisfaction with the administration and other departments/units;

2) determine if the institution is meeting its mission and quality goals;

3) reveal to the state legislators that the institution is improving in efficiency and productivity; and

4) let the employees know how well they and their unit/ department is doing.

People perform to the standards of their leaders. If management thinks people don't care then they won't care.
Philip B. Crosby

Second, the employees should also be informed that most of the measurements will be done by their department/unit and will be relevant to their needs as well as the needs of their customers. They should also be informed that the measurements will be simple, understandable, and few in number. The measurements will be done by all departments and divisions, beginning with top management (if not previously done). Because gathering baseline data is valuable as a means of taking a picture of the system, it must include all parts of the organization.

Third, the employees must see that management is committed to quality. Managers must participate in the same kinds of self-examination required of employees. They must be involved in measuring their own effectiveness and making honest judgments from the data.

Fourth, employees will see how the data is used to identify processes and procedures that could be done better and more efficiently. These suggestions are turned over to quality improvement teams and action-oriented task forces to develop corrective action.

Another benefit of combining corrective action with empowerment and trust is that employees feel encouraged to conduct self-directed assessment and to constantly improve their job performance so that things can be done quicker, better and less expensively.

If Conger and Kanungo's (1988) definition of empowerment is accepted as

> *. . . a process of enhancing feelings of self-efficacy among organizational members through the identification of conditions that foster powerlessness and through their removal by both formal organizational practices and informal techniques of providing efficacy information, ...*

then you can extend the trust approach to the level of the individual. Trust and empowerment, therefore, are more than participative management; they are directly involved in self-leadership skill development where one makes decisions and takes action on the best way to solve a problem—especially problems associated with their job. If people feel powerless, on the other hand, they will do as little as possible to maintain their job. Quality will be valued to the lowest common denominator.

Involve everyone and keep it simple

Gather data? That sounds simple enough. It should be, but you may find some objections. Many managers at universities claim that much of what they do is not measurable. That's not really accurate. After all, virtually every institution conducts annual evaluations, although they are, for the most part, statistically invalid. Besides, if the processes and systems that managers control cannot be measured, then how are managers to know when they improved a system? The purpose of measuring is not to inspect or to cause fear, but to point out dysfunctional processes and systems that can be improved.

As with managers, the faculty are evaluated routinely in their teaching (rather than whether their students are learning), research, and service abilities. Unfortunately, most institutions of higher education use methods that are not statistically significant and usually end up frightening instructors (thought-leaders) rather than providing them with an opportunity for improvement. That contradicts the goal of gathering data, which is to provide a standard from which quality can develop.

Get training on Malcolm Baldrige Award Criteria

In our book *Quality Indices: Self-Assessment Rating Instrument for Educational Institutions* (13), we suggest an evaluation and scoring procedure for determining a **quality index** (QI) for institutions of higher education. We recommended that teaching, administration, and academic affairs be evaluated separately by using a modified tool based on the Malcolm Baldrige National Quality Award Education Pilot Criteria.

The purpose of the QI tool is to suggest an expeditious method to obtain a baseline from which to begin to gather measurement data for a Continuous Quality Improvement program. It should be noted that the suggested method can be used to rate either an entire institution, or a single department/unit.

For a comprehensive look at the Baldrige Criteria and how they can be applied to evaluating your institution, you should read the excellent work of Seymour and Associates (1996).

Establish an accounting procedure

Crosby (1984, p. 110) recommends that institutions develop a cost accounting method so all procedures can be consistently measured in the same manner. That's important because colleges and universities often measure head count, cost per student credit hour, cost per full-time equivalent student, cost per major, etc. in entirely different ways. In fact, comparison between institutions sometimes becomes nearly impossible, even between institutions in the same public system. Moreover, data between departments in the same institution may be entered and interpreted in different ways.

Gathering, interpreting, and using appropriate data were major shortcomings for educational institutions that submitted applications for the first Malcolm Baldrige National Quality Award Education Pilot in 1995.

Collect and plot cost of non-conformance data

Deming believed that having quotas and numerical goals impedes quality more than any other single working condition. Yet, entire academic units are funded on student enrollments and other items such as the size of the physical plant and amount of equipment. Within a given institution, the budget may be allocated to the academic departments based entirely on the student credit hours generated, rather than the quality of the graduate.

To eliminate quotas and numerical goals, the leadership must constantly measure cost of quality and the cost of non-conformance (CON). Then, after the data is collected, it should be graphed and placed in areas for everyone to see. **Remember, the purpose of determining the CON data and plotting it is not to drive in fear, but to let people know where the institutional processes and systems are at the present time and in what direction they are headed.**

In summary, the first step to implementing CQI in an institution of higher education is to educate the management. The second step is to have management take a leadership role by making a firm commitment towards CQI. The third step is to establish quality awareness throughout the institution by having the employees educated in CQI, establishing quality advisory councils and quality improvement teams. The fourth step is to take measurements on all performances, processes, and procedures. Then the methods for measuring the cost of quality have to be standardized and the cost of quality and non-conformance have to be determined for all major processes and systems, and the results should be displayed graphically.

*Set
Goals*

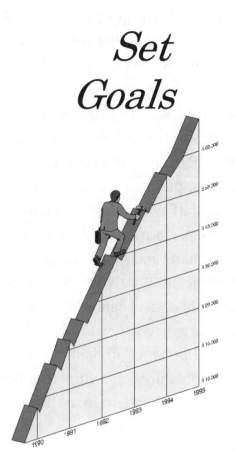

**Goals are designed to be measurable and to give you a clear picture whether or not you have achieved them.
Robert A. Cornesky**

oal setting, according to Crosby (1984, p. 116), is something that happens when the organization begins to gather data in order to measure improvements. Of course, data is needed by any institution to establish a baseline of performance. Too many institutions lack sufficient information. Then they don't adequately allocate the funds necessary to implement the plan. As a result, administrators, faculty, staff and alumni eventually can't determine how well they performed to meet the goals.

We recommend that charts and graphs displaying baseline data as well as projected goals be posted in every department. For example, historical data of student retention rates may demonstrate that a certain department has an attrition rate of 15 percent. After better advising, testing, mentoring, and tutoring procedures are implemented, the department may experience a decrease in the attrition rates over the next three years.

In summary, the first step to implementing CQI in an institution of higher education is to educate the management. The second step is to have management take a leadership role by making a firm commitment towards CQI. The third step is to establish quality awareness throughout the institution by having the employees educated in CQI, establishing quality advisory councils and quality improvement teams. The fourth step is to take measurements on all performances, processes, and procedures. Then the methods for measuring the cost of quality have to be standardized and the cost of quality and non-conformance have to be determined for all major processes and systems, and the results should be displayed graphically. The fifth step is to define unit, department, and institutional goals based on the data collected then to have the quality improvement teams take corrective action steps in removing causes of errors in processes and systems.

Good things happen only when planned; bad things happen on their own.
Philip B. Crosby

People seldom improve when they have no other model but themselves to copy after.

Goldsmith

CHAPTER SIX

Establish A Recognition Program

nstituting a recognition day could take considerable time. It might take more than two years or so after the quality processes are instituted. During planning for the recognition day, we suggest that you include representatives from major suppliers (high schools and community colleges) and customers (employers) as well as people from outside the institution (members of the governing board, labor unions, etc.). In addition to including faculty, staff, and administration in the planning process, the President should invite participants from major student-based organizations, as well as their parents and political representatives from the city or region.

Both Crosby (1984, p. 119) and Deming believe that merit pay is a very bad form of recognition. Crosby, however, believes that a serious recognition program for good employees should be created since it is a very important part of the quality movement. Crosby did his recognition awards at an annual black-tie picnic.

We believe that merit pay in institutions of higher education is an inexpensive way of getting everyone in the organization mad at each other. On the other hand, we believe that recognizing individuals and groups for efforts in establishing and/or improving quality should be done annually. As Dean of the School of Science, Management & Technologies at Edinboro University of Pennsylvania, I developed a highly successful annual quality awards dinner in which the following awards were distributed in order of **increasing importance:**

1) Best researcher (least important),
2) Best provider of community service,
3) Best innovator,
4) Best teacher, and
5) Best academic department (most important).

Whereas nominations for the best researcher, service provider, innovator, and teacher should be nominated by the faculty, we believe that the school Dean should make the final selection for the academic unit. The best academic department should be determined by predetermined criteria. We suggest using the Malcolm Baldrige National Quality Award Education Pilot Criteria. Every member of the best academic department should be awarded a "Quality" pin (as should the individual winners). The department award should be an eloquent, display-worthy placard or sculpture. The awards ceremony should occur at the University's annual quality retreat. We recommend that the institution establish such recognition ceremonies and that the ceremonies be presided over by the President.

In summary, the first step to implementing CQI in an institution of higher education is to educate the management. The second step is to have management take a leadership role by making a firm commitment towards CQI. The third step is to establish quality awareness throughout the institution by having the employees educated in CQI, establishing quality advisory councils and quality improvement teams. The fourth step is to take measurements on all performances, processes, and procedures. Then the methods for measuring the cost of quality have to be standardized and the cost of quality and non-conformance have to be determined for all major processes and systems, and the results should be displayed graphically. The fifth step is to define unit, department, and institutional goals based on the data collected then to have the quality improvement teams take corrective action steps in removing causes of errors in processes and systems. The sixth step is to recognize those individuals, teams and units/departments that have done an outstanding job in identifying process problems and in taking corrective action(s) to eliminate their occurrences. The final step is to do it over again, and again......

> **Relationships
> are where it all comes
> together or comes apart.
> Nothing else
> can be made to happen
> if relationships
> do not exist.**
>   **Philip B. Crosby**

SUGGESTED READINGS

SUGGESTED READINGS

1. Barker, Joel. *Future Edge: Discovering the New Paradigms of Success*. NY: Wm. Morrow & Co., Inc., 1992.

2. Boedecker, Ray F. *Eleven Conditions for Excellence: The IBM Total Quality Improvement Process*. Boston: American Institute of Management, 1989.

3. Bok, Derek. *Universities and the Future of America*. Durham, NC: Duke University Press, 1990.

4. Brigham, Steve et. al. *CQI 101: A First Reader for Higher Education*. Washington, DC: AAHE CQI Project, 1994.

5. Brigham, Steve et. al. *25 Snapshots of a Movement: Profiles of Campuses Implementing CQI*. Washington, DC: AAHE CQI Project, 1994.

6. Conger, Jay and Rabindra Kanungo. *The Empowerment Process: Integrating Theory and Practice*. Academy of Management Review, July 1988.

SUGGESTED READINGS

7. Cornesky, Robert A., Ron Baker, Cathy Cavanaugh, William Etling, Michael Lukert, Sam McCool, Brian McKay, An-Sik Min, Charlotte Paul, Paul Thomas, David Wagner, and John Darling. *Using Deming to Improve Quality in Colleges and Universities*, Madison, WI: Magna Publications, Inc., 1989.

8. Cornesky, Robert A., Sam McCool, Larry Byrnes, and Robert Weber. *Implementing Total Quality Management in Institutions of Higher Education.* Madison, WI: Magna Publications, Inc., 1991.

9   Cornesky, Robert A. and Sam McCool. *Total Quality Improvement Guide for Institutions of Higher Education.* Madison, WI: Magna Publications, Inc., 1992.

10. Cornesky, Robert A. *The Quality Professor: Implementing Total Quality Management in the College Classroom.* Madison, WI: Magna Publications, Inc., 1993.

11. Cornesky, Robert and William Lazarus. *Continuous Quality Improvement in the Classroom: A Collaborative Approach.* Cornesky & Associates, Inc., 1995.

SUGGESTED READINGS

12. Cornesky, Robert A. *Turning Continuous Quality Improvement Into Institutional Practice: The Tools and Techniques*. Port Orange, FL: Cornesky & Associates, Inc. 1995.

13. Cornesky, Robert A. *Quality Indices: Self-Assessment Rating Instrument for Educational Institutions*. Port Orange, FL: Cornesky & Associates, Inc. 1995.

14. Covey, Stephen R. *The 7 Habits of Highly Effective People*. NY: Simon & Schuster, 1989.

15. Crosby, Philip B. *Quality Without Tears: The Art of Hassle-Free Management*. New York: McGraw-Hill Book Co., 1984.

16. Crosby, Philip B. *Let's Talk Quality*. New York: McGraw-Hill Book Co., 1989.

17. Deal, T.E. and A.A. Kennedy, *Corporate Culture*. Reading, MA: Addison-Wesley, 1982.

18. De Man, Henri. *Joy in Work*. Trans. Eden and Cedar Paul (from the German). London: George Allen & Unwin, 1939.

SUGGESTED READINGS

19. Deming, W. Edwards. *Out of the Crisis*. Cambridge, MA: Productivity Press or Washington, DC: The George Washington University, MIT-CAES, 1982.

20. Ferguson, Marilyn. *The Aquarian Conspiracy*. Boston: Houghton Mifflin Co., 1980.

21. Gardner, John W. *On Leadership*. New York: The Free Press, 1990.

22. Hrebiniak, Lawrence G. *Complex Organizations*. New York: West Publishing Co., 1978.

23. Hubbard, Dean L. *Continuous Quality Improvement: Making the Transition to Education*. Maryville: Prescott Publishing Company, 1993.

24. Imai, Masaaki. *Kaizen: The Key to Japan's Competitive Success*. Cambridge, MA: Productivity Press, 1986.

25. Ishikawa, Kaoru. *Guide to Quality Control*. Englewood Cliffs, NJ: Prentice Hall, 1982.

26. Johnston, William B. *Workforce 2000: Work and Workers in the Twenty-First Century* Indianapolis, Ind.: Hudson Institute, 1987.

SUGGESTED READINGS

27. Juran, J.M. *Juran On Planning For Quality*. Cambridge, MA: Productivity Press, 1988.

28. Katz, D., and R. L. Kahn. *The Social Psychology of Organizations*. New York: John Wiley & Sons, Inc., 1966.

29. Kilmann, Ralph H. "Corporate Culture." *Psychology Today* April 1985.

30. Levering, Robert. *A Great Place to Work*. New York: Random House, Inc., 1988.

31. Manz, Charles C., and Henry P. Sims, Jr. *Super-Leadership*. New York: The Berkeley Publishing Group, 1990.

32. Millett, John D. *The Academic Community*. New York: McGraw-Hill, 1962.

33. Mitra, Amitava. *Fundamentals of Quality Control Improvement*. New York: Macmillan Publishing Company, 1993.

34. Norman, Colin. "Rethinking Technology's Role in Economic Change," *Science* (May 20, 1988): 977.

SUGGESTED READINGS

35. Peters, Tom and Nancy Austin. *A Passion for Excellence*. New York: Random House, Inc., 1985.

36. Peters, Tom. *Thriving on Chaos*. New York: Harper & Row, 1988.

37. Roberts, Keith and James B. Rieley. *Institutional Effectiveness*. Milwaukee: The Center for Continuous Quality Improvement, Milwaukee Area Technical College, 1995.

38. Sarazen, Stephen. *The Tools of Quality Part II: Cause-and-Effect Diagrams*. Quality Progress, July 1990.

39. Seymour, Daniel. *Once Upon a Campus: Lessons for Improving Quality and Productivity in Higher Education*. Phoenix: The Orynx Press, 1995.

40. Seymour, Daniel. *The AQC Baldrige Report: Lessons Learned By Nine Colleges and Universities Undertaking Self-Study With the Malcolm Baldrige National Quality Award Criteria*. Academic Quality Consortium. A Project of the American Association for Higher Education, 1996.

SUGGESTED READINGS

41. Seymour, Daniel and Associates. *The Malcolm Baldrige National Quality Award as a Framework for Improving Higher Education. Volume I: Theory and Concepts. Volume II: Case and Practice.* Maryville, MO: Prescott Publishing Company, 1996.

42. Walton, Mary. *The Deming Management Method.* New York: The Putnam Publishing Group, 1986.

43. Waterman, Robert H. *Adhocracy: The Power to Change.* Knoxville, TN: Whittle Direct Books, 1990.

For more information on the following publications, or to order contact:

CORNESKY & ASSOCIATES, INC.
489 Oakland Park Blvd.
Port Orange, FL 32127-9538

PHONE:

(800) 388-8682
or
(904) 760-5866

FAX:

(904) 756-6755

E-MAIL:

TQM1BOB@AOL.COM

The Chronicle of CQI

The Latest News On Continuous Quality Improvement In Education

June 1996 Vol. 2 No. 4

The Chronicle of CQI is published by Cornesky & Associates, Inc., Total Quality Management consultants and publishers for educational institutions. For information call (800) 388-8682 or (904) 760-5866; fax (904) 756-6755; E-mail: tqm1bob@aol.com

PENN STATE'S DEPARTMENT OF PURCHASING DEALS A QUALITY HAND

by Karen I. Wagner, Manager,
Marketing and Customer Service

While trying to improve its purchasing process, Penn State University found itself holding all the cards. So, it plans to deal them out later this year in one of several new programs generated by Continuous Quality Improvement teams to improve purchasing-related processes.

It's been all uses for the Procurement Card Program, which should be in place sometime after July. "It will offer faculty and staff the ease and convenience of credit-card based transactions with reduced paperwork processing and lead time," explains Betty Roberts, Assistant Vice President for Business Services.

The card were developed to improve and streamline the process of acquiring non-strategic, low-dollar purchases. Pre-approved employees would be empowered to handle purchases for up to $1,000 per transaction. The program will improve efficiencies while giving the user direct contact with the supplier, Roberts says.

Meanwhile, she points out, the University will be able to consolidate and better manage its buying agreements, and better monitor contract compliance.

From the vendor's perspective, the Procurement Card will result in faster payment with reduced billing and collection costs. And a vendor will only have to contact one person to resolve any problems.

The University began to shuffle the deck by creating a University Task Force to determine the benefit of developing a Procurement Card program and identify appropriate benchmarks. The task force consisted of representatives from Purchasing Services, University financial officers, Computer Information Systems, Systems and Procedures, Accounting Operations, Hershey Medical Center, and the University's auditors.

Through a series of focus interviews with faculty and staff members, the task force evaluated the potential benefits of the program. In addition, the committee also benchmarked Big Ten universities and other institutions that are already using procurement cards.

No employee has actually been dealt the card yet. The University is still developing the idea and evaluating responses from the interviews. Another cross-functional design team is formulating the new electronic procedures and guidelines. A banking partner will then be selected before the cards are distributed, Roberts says.

"Although we can't say at this point what if any actual dollar savings will accrue to the institution, we believe the newly streamlined process will significantly reduce processing time," she says.

The cards are just one part of planned improvements in the University's audit/control process. Purchasing has also put together a Reengineering Team to re-examine the purchasing process in general. The objective of this CQI team is to transform the process, so the University can save money by reducing individual purchases and increasing volume buying.

To ensure any solution is customer-driven, the team will be soliciting direct input from the high-volume users of support units—the auxiliary enterprises.

Penn State continued on page 2

"The program will improve efficiencies while giving the user direct contact with the supplier."

Karen I. Wagner

Betty Roberts

The Chronicle of CQI newsletter is based on the **Malcolm Baldrige National Quality Award Education Pilot Criteria**. It gives you tips and techniques on continuous quality improvement for schools, colleges, and universities. You'll find feature stories, first-person reports, news accounts and updates on how professors and administrators worldwide are using CQI to resolve their difficult problems—problems similar to the ones facing you and your institution. You'll learn: How to save money while increasing productivity and quality of service; how to implement CQI/TQM at your campus and in your classrooms; how to boost morale among faculty, staff, and students; how to improve retention; how to use CQI tools to assess your progress and build consensus; and much more.

Robert A. Cornesky, editor • $79 per year (11 issues) • Foreign Subscriptions Call for Price Quotes

There are a limited number of back issues, please call for price and availability.

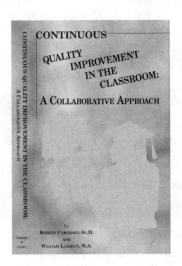

Continuous Quality Improvement in the Classroom: A Collaborative Approach

Robert A. Cornesky, Sc.D. and William Lazarus, M.A.

The authors use a "systems" approach as the core for their eleven step training program. They examine the classroom from four systems: 1) the **facilitation** system, 2) the **learning** system, 3) the **improvement** system, and 4) the **payment** (or reward) system. They call the model **CQI Action**. The book contains a self-assessment of teaching effectiveness tool based on the Malcolm Baldrige National Quality Award Education Pilot Criteria and 15 continuous quality improvement tools and techniques for effective teaching.

1st Printing August 1995 • Approx. 290 pages • $38 S&H included • ISBN 1-881807-08-8

Turning Continuous Quality Improvement into Institutional Practice: The Tools and Techniques

Robert A. Cornesky, Sc.D.

This manual is for managers in education. It is divided into three sections. The first section presents the commonalties in the approaches and principles to continuous quality improvement (CQI). The second section presents versions of self-assessment quality profile index tools based on the Malcolm Baldrige National Quality Award Education Pilot Criteria. There is a self-assessment for the classroom teaching and learning systems, another for the academic support systems, and one for the administrative support systems. These data should provide you with information on where your various units should most likely begin their quality journey. The third section describes a cooperative model based on the plan-do-check-act cycle. It shows how to define the quality problems of a department, gives some pointers on how to establish quality improvement teams, and walks you through the steps that have to be taken to conduct the improvement study and to recommend solutions to your quality problems. The appendix describes many of the continuous quality improvement tools and techniques that you will find invaluable in beginning your quality journey.

1st Printing August 1995 • Approx. 150 Pages • $30 S&H included • ISBN 1-881807-09-6

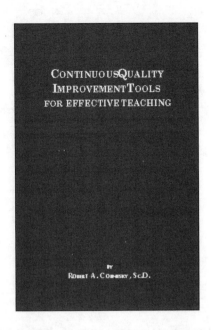

Continuous Quality Improvement Tools for Effective Teaching
Robert A. Cornesky, Sc.D.
The author presents the 15 continuous quality improvement (CQI) tools and techniques necessary for effective teaching. By using the tools and techniques of continuous quality improvement , teachers will be able to help themselves and their students to focus on the classroom processes. This will permit the teacher and students to plan, organize, implement, and make decisions about learning.
1st Printing September 1995 • Approx. 160 Pages • $30.00 S&H included • ISBN 1-881807-07-X

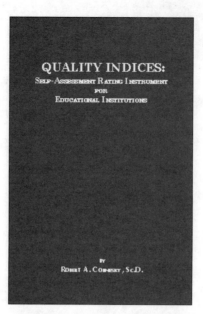

Quality Indices: Self-Assessment Rating Instrument for Educational Institutions
Robert A. Cornesky, Sc.D.
This quality index survey instrument is based on the Malcolm Baldrige National Quality Award Education Pilot Criteria (MBNQA). Also included is a Macintosh based, Works™ 3.0 and PC Windows Works™ programmed diskette containing the self-scoring instruments. The author developed this instrument to familiarize educators with the intricacies of the MBNQA Criteria by providing them with a diagnostic instrument that measures the quality of their institutional processes and systems, and to provide a method for getting an approximate quality baseline of institutional services and products in the various units before a continuous quality improvement effort is undertaken. The instrument is divided into three self-assessment parts, each of which evaluates the processes and systems of a different functional unit of the educational institution: 1) Classroom Teaching and Learning, 2) Academic Support, and 3) Administrative Support. To get an institutional rating the three individual unit scores must be considered.
1st Printing July 1995 • Approx. 40 Pages with Disk • $23 S&H included • ISBN 1-881807-10-X

Turning
Total Quality Management
into
Classroom Practice

by
Margaret A. Byrnes, Ed.S.
and
Robert A. Cornesky, Sc.D.

Quality Fusion: Turning Total Quality Management into Classroom Practice

Margaret A. Byrnes and Robert A. Cornesky

The authors carefully elaborate on eleven sequential steps for turning TQM into classroom practice for K-12 teachers. They use an approach that actively involves the students as they meet "customer" expectations, including parent, employer, and the instructor down the line. While teachers master the art of coaching, students learn the joy of discovery! Used by many colleges and school of education as a text.

3rd Printing June 1995 • 294 Pages • $22.50 S&H included • ISBN 1-881807-05-03

Implementing
Total Quality Management
in the Classroom

by
Margaret A. Byrnes, Ed.S.
Robert A. Cornesky, Sc.D.
and
Lawrence W. Byrnes, Ph.D.

The Quality Teacher: Implementing Total Quality Management in the Classroom
Margaret A. Byrnes, Robert A. Cornesky, and Lawrence W. Byrnes
This book is an international best seller and is a practical guide that shows you how to use the TQM approaches of Dr. Deming and others in the classroom, and how total quality improvement tools can be used with the students, including those that are at-risk. The book also contains a **Personal Quality Index** form based on the Malcolm Baldrige National Quality Award Criteria.
6th Printing June 1995 • 337 Pages • $22.50 S&H included • ISBN 1-881807-01-0

For more information about these
publications, or to order contact:

CORNESKY & ASSOCIATES, INC.
489 Oakland Park Blvd.
Port Orange, FL 32127-9538

PHONE:

(800) 388-8682
or
(904) 760-5866

FAX:

(904) 756-6755

E-MAIL:

TQM1BOB@AOL.COM

ROBERT CORNESKY was the first to apply what is known as Total Quality Management (TQM) to the administration of colleges and universities, including the classroom. He was the first to publish a book on applying TQM to academic settings. From 1987 to 1991, Dr. Cornesky served as the Dean of the School of Science, Management & Technologies at  Edinboro University of Pennsylvania. From 1982 to 1987, he served as the Dean of the School of Allied Health at Texas Tech University Health Sciences Center where he also served as Professor and the Director of Telenetworking. As a college professor and administrator since 1964, he has also been associated with Governors State University in Illinois (University Professor and Director of the School of Health Related Professions), with California State University—Bakersfield (Professor of Biology and Health Sciences; Chair, Department of Health Sciences), and with Carnegie-Mellon University (Assistant Professor, Department of Biological Sciences).

Since 1991, Dr. Cornesky has served as President of his own consulting and publishing firm which specializes in providing TQM services to educational institutions. He was the founding editor of the *TQM in Higher Education* newsletter and is the editor of *The Chronicle of CQI* a newsletter for Continuous Quality Improvement in Education.